Mom &
Dad —

book ... beautiful
for you two
to share.

Thank-You
so very
much.

Love,
Sarah.

Apples of Gold

A word fitly spoken
is like apples of gold
in pictures of silver.

Proverbs 25:11

Apples of Gold

Compiled by Jo Petty

Published by The C. R. Gibson Company

Norwalk, Connecticut

But the fruit of the Spirit is love,
joy, peace, long suffering, gentleness,
goodness, faith, meekness, temperance:
against such there is no law.

Galatians 5:22-23

Contents

The material in this book has
been collected over a long period
of time. Many of the original
sources are unknown to the compiler.
The compiler wishes to acknowledge
the original authors, whoever they
may be, but has confidence that
they would urge, with her, "Do not
inquire as to who said this, but
pay attention to what is said."

Love

Scientists know only what love does. Love, properly applied, could virtually empty our asylums, our prisons, our hospitals. Love is the touchstone of psychiatric treatment. Love can be fostered, extended, used to subjugate hate and thus cure diseases. More and more clearly every day, out of biology, anthropology, sociology, history, economics, psychology, the plain common sense, the necessary mandate of survival—that we love our neighbors as ourselves— is being confirmed and reaffirmed. Christ gave us only one commandment—Love . . . Now to the laboratory with love!

Where love is, there God is.

To love is virtually to know; to know is not virtually to love.

Real friends are those who, when you've made a fool of yourself, don't feel that you've done a permanent job.

We may give without loving, but we cannot love without giving.

Work is love made visible.

It also takes two to make up after a quarrel.

Faults are thick when love is thin.

To love life through labor is to be intimate with life's inmost secret.

Do not judge your friend until you stand in his place.

He who sows courtesy reaps friendship, and he who plants kindness gathers love.

You shall judge a man by his foes as well as by his friends.

Adolescence is the age at which children stop asking questions because they know all the answers.

Except in occasional emergencies there is not much that one man can do for another, other than to help him to help himself.

The door to the human heart can be opened only from the inside.

Friendship is to be purchased only by friendship.

Let us be the first to give a friendly sign, to nod first, smile first, speak first, and— if such a thing is necessary—forgive first.

The light of friendship is like the light of
phosphorus, seen when all around is dark.

I did a favor yesterday,
　　A kindly little deed . . .
And then I called to all the world
　　To stop and look and heed.
They stopped and looked and flattered me
　　In words I could not trust,
And when the world had gone away
　　My good deed turned to dust.

A very tiny courtesy
　　I found to do today;
'Twas quickly done, with none to see,
　　And then I ran away . . .
But Someone must have witnessed it,
　　For—truly I declare—
As I sped back the stony path
　　Roses were blooming there!

Restraint without love is barbarity.
Love without restraint commits suicide.

For we must share if we would keep
　　That blessing from above;
Ceasing to give, we cease to have,
　　Such is the law of love.

If a single man achieves the highest kind
of love, it will be sufficient to neutralize
the hate of millions.

Love cannot be wasted. It makes no
difference where it is bestowed, it always
brings in big returns.

God pardons like a mother, who kisses the
offense into everlasting forgetfulness.

To handle yourself, use your head;
To handle others, use your heart.

Measure your life by loss instead of gain;
not by the wine drunk, but in the wine
poured forth, for love's strength
stands in love's sacrifice; and who suffers
most has most to give.

The only safe and sure way to destroy an
enemy is to make him your friend.

Are you lonely, O my brother?
Share your little with another!
Stretch a hand to one unfriended,
And your loneliness is ended.

The only greatness is unselfish love.

Return to him who does you wrong your purest
love, and he will cease from doing wrong; for
love will purify the heart of him who is beloved
as truly as it purifies the heart of him who loves.

Creation of woman from the rib of man:
She was not made of his head to top him;
nor out of his feet to be trampled upon
by him; but out of his side to be equal
with him; under his arm, to be protected;
and near his heart to be beloved.

A foreigner is a friend I haven't met yet.

The only way to have a friend is to be one.

It is only the forgiving who are qualified
to receive forgiveness.

The father is the head of the house—
The mother is the heart of the house.

The love you liberate in your work
is the love you keep.

How seldom we weigh our neighbor in
the same balance with ourselves.

A friend is a person with whom you dare
to be yourself.

Add all the love of all the parents and
the total sum cannot be multiplied enough
times to express God's love for me, the
least of his children.

A long life is barely enough for a man
and a woman to understand each other; and
to be understood is to love. The man who
understands one woman is qualified to
understand pretty well everything.

> Not the quarry, but the chase,
> Not the trophy, but the race.

Love is not soft like water, it is hard like rock,
on which the waves of hatred beat in vain.

It is in loving, not in being loved, the heart
is blessed; It is in giving, not in seeking gifts,
we find our quest; Whatever be your longing
or your need, that give; So shall your soul
be fed, and you indeed shall live.

To learn and never be filled, is wisdom;
To teach and never be weary is love.

Conscience is God's presence in man.

Mrs.—Do you love me still?
Mr.—Yes, better than any other way.

God regards the greatness of the love that
prompts the man, rather than the greatness
of his achievement.

It is as absurd to pretend that one cannot love
the same woman always as to pretend that a good
artist needs several violins to play a piece of music.

I married her because we have so many
faults in common.

We like someone because. We love someone although.

A friend is one who knows all about you
and still likes you.

Go often to the house of your friend, for
weeds choke up the unused path.

Your friend has a friend, and your friend's friend
has a friend; be discreet.

He that cannot forgive others breaks the bridge
over which he must pass, for every man has
need to be forgiven.

Forgiveness is the fragrance the violet sheds
on the heel that crushed it.

To understand is to pardon.

Friendship is the only cement that will
ever hold the world together.

Always forgive your enemies; nothing annoys
them so much.

Love is the passionate and abiding desire on
the part of two or more people to produce
together conditions under which each can
be, and spontaneously express, his real self;
to produce together an intellectual soil and an
emotional climate in which each can flourish,
far superior to what either could achieve alone.

The best way for a husband to clinch an
argument is to take her in his arms.

The bonds of matrimony aren't worth much
unless the interest is kept up.

A friend is a present you give yourself.

One reason why a dog is such a lovable crea-
ture is that his tail wags instead of his tongue.

Come what may, hold fast to *love*! Though
men should rend your heart, let them not
embitter or harden it. We win by tenderness;
we conquer by forgiveness.

One of the mysteries of life is how the
boy who wasn't good enough to marry the
daughter can be the father of the smartest
grandchild in the world.

Friends are made by many acts—and
lost by only one.

Pure religion is love in action.

The smallest good deed is better than
the grandest intention.

> I've found a little remedy
>   To ease the life we live
> And make each day a happier one—
>   It is the word 'forgive'.
>
> So often little things come up
>   That leave a pain and sting,
> That covered up at once would not
>   Amount to anything.
>
> 'Tis when we hold them up to view,
>   And brood and sulk and fret,
> They greater grow before our eyes;
>   'Twere better to forget.

Politeness is a small price to pay for the
good will and affection of others.

The greater the man, the greater the courtesy.

The coin of God's realm is love.

A partnership with God is motherhood.

It is better to have loved and lost than never
to have loved at all.

American Creed: Patriotism which
leaps over the fence of party prejudice.
Religion which jumps over the wall of intoler-
ance. Brotherhood which climbs over the
mountain of national separations.

The best gifts are tied with heartstrings.

Man is probably the only animal which even
attempts to have anything to do with his
half-grown young.

Every calling is great when greatly pursued.

An injurious truth has no merit over an injurious lie.

A friend is one who comes to you when
all others leave.

> He drew a circle that shut me out,
> But love and I had the wit to win;
> We drew a larger circle that took him in.

Mothers, as well as fools, sometimes walk
where angels fear to tread.

When a man does a noble act, date him from
that. Forget his faults. Let his noble act be the
standpoint from which you regard him.

A mistake at least proves somebody stopped
talking long enough to do something.

A teacher affects eternity; he can never tell
where his influence stops.

'Twas her thinking of others made you think of her.

Water which is distant is no good for a
fire which is near.

Success in marriage is much more than
finding the right person; it is a matter of
being the right person.

Hate is a prolonged manner of suicide.

Some women work so hard to make good husbands that they never quite manage to make good wives.

Put yourself in his place.

What counts is not the number of hours you put in, but how much you put in the hours.

Love sees through a telescope—not a microscope.

Some people give and forgive; others get and forget.

He makes no friends who never made a foe.

Women's styles may change, but their designs remain the same.

If you had to do it over, would you fall in love with yourself again?

A woman worries about the future until she gets a husband, while a man never worries about the future until he gets a wife.

Ceremonies are different in every country, but true politeness is everywhere the same.

Joy

There is nothing I can give you which you have
not, but there is much that while I cannot
give you, you can take:
No heaven can come to us unless our hearts find
rest in it today. Take Heaven.
No peace lies in the future which is not hidden
in this present instant. Take Peace.
The gloom of the world is but a shadow;
behind it, yet within reach, is joy. Take Joy.

It is easy to be pleasant
    When life flows by like a song,
But the man worth while is one who will smile,
    When everything goes dead wrong.

For the test of the heart is trouble,
    And it always comes with the years,
And the smile that is worth the praises of earth
    Is the smile that shines thru the tears.

Keep your enthusiasms, and forget your birthdays—
formula for youth!

Do you see *difficulties* in every *opportunity*
or *opportunities* in every *difficulty*?

If you would know the greatest sum in addition,
count your blessings.

Money and time are the heaviest burdens of life,
and the unhappiest of all mortals are those who
have more of either than they know how to use.

I can alter my life by altering my attitude of mind.

As torrents in summer, half dried in their channels,
Suddenly rise, 'tho the sky is still cloudless,
For rain has been falling far off at their fountains;
So hearts that are fainting grow full to o'erflowing,
And they that behold it marvel, and know not
That God at their fountains, so far off has been raining.

Happiness is possible only when one is
busy. The body must toil, the mind
must be occupied, and the heart must be
satisfied. Those who do good as opportunity
offers are sowing seed all the time, and they
need not doubt the harvest.

> Joy, temperance and repose
> Slam the door on the doctor's nose.

One of the great arts of living is the art
of forgetting.

He who would have nothing to do with thorns
must never attempt to gather flowers.

Don't let the seeds spoil your enjoyment of a
watermelon. Just spit out the seeds.

Little and often fills the purse.

You grow up the day you have your first
real laugh—at yourself.

There is no place more delightful than
one's own fireside.

When shall we all learn that the *good news* needs
the telling, and that all men need to know?

Keep on your toes and you won't
run down at the heels.

Interesting people are people who are interested.
Bores are people who are bored.

Yes, it's pretty hard, the optimistic old
woman admitted. I have to get along with
only two teeth—one upper, one lower—but,
thank goodness, they meet.

Some cause happiness wherever they go;
others whenever they go.

Happiness is a perfume you cannot pour on
others without getting a few drops on yourself.

I'm so glad I'm back home I'm glad I went.

I do not feel any age yet. There is
no age to the spirit.

To what avail the plow or sail, or land,
or life, if freedom fail?

To be without some of the things you want
is an indispensable part of happiness.

There are no uninteresting things, there are
only uninteresting people.

I want a soul so full of joy—
Life's withering storms cannot destroy.

Diner: 'Do you serve crabs here?'
Waiter: 'We serve anyone; sit down.'

The worst bankrupt in the world is the man
who has lost his enthusiasm. Let him lose
everything but enthusiasm and he will come
through again to success.

I have noticed that folks are generally about
as happy as they have made up their minds to be.

If you want to be happy,
   Begin where you are,
Don't wait for some rapture
   That's future and far.
Begin to be joyous, begin to be glad
   And soon you'll forget
That you ever were sad.

Two tragedies in life: One is not to get your
heart's desire. The other is to get it.

For all its terrors and tragedies . . .
the life of man is a thing of potential beauty
and dignity . . . To live is good.

I know what happiness is, for I have
done good work.

Growing old is no more than a bad habit
which a busy person has no time to form.

The only consistently bright life is the
persistently right life.

What one has, one ought to use; and whatever
he does he should do with all his might.

> One day as I sat musing
> Alone and melancholy and without a friend,
> There came a voice from out of the gloom,
> Saying, 'Cheer up! Things might be worse.'
> So I cheered up,
> And sure enough—things got worse.

It takes both rain and sunshine to make a rainbow.

God does not deduct from man's allotted time
those hours spent in *fishing*.

An unfailing mark of a blockhead is the chip
on his shoulder.

Keep ascending the mountain of cheerfulness
by daily scattering seeds of kindness along
the way as best you can, and, should mists hide
the mountaintop, continue undaunted and
you will reach the sun-tipped heights in
your own life-experience.

People are lonely because they build walls
instead of bridges.

Let us realize that what happens round us
is largely outside our control, but that the way
we choose to react to it is inside our control.

Any person who is always feeling sorry
for himself, should be.

All people smile in the same language.

The only way on earth to multiply happiness
is to divide it.

> How many smiles from day to day
> I've missed along my narrow way!
> How many kindly words I've lost
> What joy has my indifference cost!
> This glorious friend that now I know
> Would have been friendly years ago.

It is not he who has little, but he who
wants more, who is poor.

A man's mind is like his car. If it gets
to knocking too much, he'd better have
it overhauled or change it.

One of the best things a man can have
up his sleeve is a funny-bone.

Never miss an opportunity to make others happy,
even if you have to let them alone to do it.

Old age isn't so bad . . . when you consider
the alternative.

The really happy man is the one who can enjoy
the scenery when he has to take a detour.

Success is a bright sun that obscures and
makes ridiculously unimportant all the little
shadowy flecks of failure.

The cost of a thing is that amount of life which
must be exchanged for it.

Mirth is from God, and dullness is from
the devil. You can never be too sprightly,
you can never be too good—tempered.

Plan your work—work your plan.

Change yourself and your work will seem different.

Be cheerful. Of all the things you wear, your
expression is the most important.

To be happy ourselves is a most effectual
contribution to the happiness of others.

I am born happy every morning.

So long as enthusiasm lasts, so long is
youth still with us.

Apart from enthusiasm, joy cannot live.

The world belongs to the enthusiast
who keeps cool.

Be a lamp in the chamber if you cannot be
a star in the sky.

What sunshine is to flowers, smiles are to humanity.

If we fill our hours with regrets over the failures
of yesterday, and with worries over the
problems of tomorrow, we have no today
in which to be thankful.

Blessed is the man who digs a well from which
another may draw faith.

Spilled on this earth are all the joys of heaven.

The secret of being miserable is to have
the leisure to bother about whether
you are happy or not.

Always speak the truth and you'll never be
concerned with your memory.

There is no duty we so much underrate
as the duty of being happy.

Mind unemployed is Mind unenjoyed.

Just think how happy you'd be if you lost
everything you have right now—and then
got it back again.

Earth is crammed with heaven
And every common bush is afire with God.

>Laugh a little—sing a little
>>As you go your way!
>Work a little—play a little,
>>Do this every day!

>Give a little—take a little,
>>Never mind a frown—
>Make your smile a welcomed thing
>>All around the town!

>Laugh a little—love a little,
>>Skies are always blue!
>Every cloud has silver linings,
>>But it's up to you!

If you ever find happiness by hunting for it, you
will find it, as the old woman did her lost
spectacles, safe on her nose all the time.

Remember that the coin you clutch
has never brought happiness.
The world and you will profit more
from sincere thoughtfulness.

Happiness consists in activity—it is a running
stream, not a stagnant pool.

> They told him it couldn't be done.
>> With a smile, he went right to it.
> He tackled the thing that couldn't be done
>> And couldn't do it.

May you live all the days of your life.

When a man has a 'pet peeve' it's remarkable
how often he pets it.

The real democratic American idea is not that
every man shall be on a level with every other,
but that every man shall have liberty, without
hindrance, to be what God made him.

He who receives a benefit with gratitude
repays the first installment on his debt.

If I keep a green bough in my heart,
the singing bird will come.

You have no more right to consume happiness
without producing it than to consume wealth
without producing it.

Cold and reserved natures should remember
that, though not infrequently flowers may be
found beneath the snow, it is chilly work to
dig for them and few care to take the trouble.

Every man's work is a portrait of himself.

Economy makes happy homes and sound
nations; instill it deep.

Things are pretty well evened up in this world.
Other people's troubles are not so bad as yours,
but their children are a lot worse.

The office of government is not to confer
happiness, but to give men opportunity to
work out happiness for themselves.

If you would make a man happy, do not
add to his possessions but subtract from
the sum of his desires.

> Why help to make the world a dreary place—
> Why be a rainy day?
> Why harp on old mistakes that we regret?
> Why be a rainy day?
> Why wear the dismal mask of hopelessness?
> Why be a rainy day?

Sorrow with his pick mines the heart,
but he is a cunning workman. He deepens
the channels whereby happiness may enter,
and he hollows out new chambers for joy
to abide in, when he is gone.

Children are a great comfort in your old age—
and they help you reach it faster, too.

One great use of words is to hide our thoughts.

Praise, like gold and diamonds, owes its value
to its scarcity.

Heaven is blessed with perfect rest,
but the blessing of earth is toil.

True happiness depends upon close
alliance with God.

To see God in everything makes life the
greatest adventure there is.

A thankful heart is not only the greatest virtue,
but the parent of all the other virtues.

Humdrum is not where you live; it's what you are.

A sad saint is a sorry saint.

Happiness is the best teacher of good manners;
only the unhappy are churlish.

There is always something wrong
with a man, as there is with a motor,
when he knocks continually.

> A Smile is Cheer to you and me
> The cost is nothing—it's given free
> It comforts the weary—gladdens the sad
> Consoles those in trouble—good or bad
> To rich and poor—beggar or thief
> It's free to all of any belief
> A natural gesture of young and old
> Cheers on the faint—disarms the bold
> Unlike most blessings for which we pray
> It's one thing we keep when we give it away.

We must be willing to pay a price for freedom,
for no price that is ever asked for it is half
the cost of doing without it.

O, I am grown so free from care
since my heart broke!

Life and Death are parts of the same great
adventure. Do not fear to die and do not
shrink from the joy of life.

Sit ye, rock and think.

You may call that your own which no man
can take from you.

Optimist or Pessimist? Do you call
traffic signals go-lights?

Living is like licking honey off a thorn.

If we learn how to give ourselves, to forgive
others, and to live with thanksgiving,
we need not seek happiness—it will seek us.

Gratitude is the memory of the heart.

Sympathy is never wasted except when you
give it to yourself.

No man has more time than I.

Better to light one candle than to
curse the darkness.

The man who deals in sunshine is the man
    who wins the crowds.
He does a lot more business than the man
    who peddles clouds.

Visits always give pleasure—if not the coming,
then the going.

Liberty is always dangerous, but it is the
safest thing we have.

Winter on her head — Eternal spring in her heart.

All sunshine makes a desert.

Joy is not in things, it is in us.

Happiness is a thing to be practiced like a violin.

That load becomes light which is cheerfully borne.

Manners are the happy way of doing things.

To be wronged is nothing unless you continue
to remember it.

> Our joys are our wings;
> Our sorrows are our spurs.

The days that make us happy make us wise.

There is nothing more beautiful than a rainbow,
but it takes both rain and sunshine to make
a rainbow. If life is to be rounded and
many-colored like the rainbow, both joy and
sorrow must come to it. Those who have
never known anything but prosperity and
pleasure become hard and shallow, but those
whose prosperity has been mixed with adversity
become kind and gracious.

Almost all men improve on acquaintance.

Happiness consists not in possessing much,
but in being content with what we now
possess. He who wants little always has enough.

The smile on your face is the light in the window
that tells people that you are at home.

The secret of happy living is not to do what
you like but to like what you do.

If you don't make a living, live on what you make.

If we pause to think, we will have cause to thank.

Some men have their first dollar.
The man who is really rich
is one who still has his first friend.

> Once upon a time I planned to be
>   An artist of celebrity.
> A song I thought to write one day,
>   And all the world would homage pay.
> I longed to write a noted book,
>   But what I did was—learn to cook.
> For life with simple tasks is filled,
>   And I have done, not what I willed,
> Yet when I see boys' hungry eyes
>   I'm glad I make good apple pies!

The way to be happy is to make others happy.
Helping others is the secret of all success—
in business, in the arts and in the home.

We do not know how cheap the seeds of
happiness are or we should scatter them oftener.

To speak kindly does not hurt the tongue.

The nearer she approached the end, the plainer
she seemed to hear round her the immortal
symphonies of the world to come.

Dwell on the Duty of Happiness
as well as the Happiness of Duty.

No man ever injured his eyesight by looking
on the bright side of things.

Happiness is the only thing we can give
without having.

There is no cosmetic for beauty like *happiness*.

The secret of contentment is knowing how to
enjoy what you have and be able to lose
all desire for things beyond your reach.

Do not speak of your happiness to one
less fortunate than yourself.

Happiness is not a station you arrive at,
but a manner of traveling.

You can't keep trouble from coming, but you
needn't give it a chair to sit on.

Success is getting what you want;
Happiness is wanting what you get.

Many of us spend half our time wishing
for things we could have if we didn't spend
half our time wishing.

All the flowers of all the tomorrows are
in the seeds of today.

Defeat isn't bitter if you don't swallow it.

The deeper that sorrow carves into your being,
the more joy you can contain.

The way to be happy is to make others happy.

The blue of heaven is larger than the clouds.

I should like to spend the whole of my life
traveling, if I could anywhere borrow
another life to live at home.

It is when the holiday is over that we begin
to enjoy it.

The light that shines the farthest shines the
brightest nearest home.

The happiness of your life depends upon
the quality of your thoughts.

The glory of life is to love, not to be loved,
to give, not to get; to serve, not to be served.

> Pleasures are like poppies spread;
> You seize the flower, the bloom is shed.

One of the biggest thrills in life comes from
doing a job well.

Each new day is an opportunity to start all
over again . . . to cleanse our minds and hearts
anew and to clarify our vision. And let us not
clutter up today with the leavings of other days.

Peace

Take with you words, strong words of courage:
Words that have wings! . . .
Take with you holy words, words that know God;
Words that are sacred as healing waters,
Pure as light, and beautiful as morning,
Take with you tall words, words that reach up,
And growing words, with deep life within them.
Take with you holy words, words that know God.

In His will is our peace.

If there is righteousness in the heart,
    there will be beauty in the character,
If there is beauty in the character,
    there will be harmony in the home.
If there is harmony in the home,
    there will be order in the nation,
If there is order in the nation,
    there will be peace in the world.

Man's capacity for justice makes democracy
possible; but man's inclination to injustice
makes democracy necessary.

Fear God and all other fears will disappear.

In much of my talking, thinking is half-murdered.

If you clutter up your mind with little things,
will there be any room left for the big things?

We can never herd the world into the paths of
righteousness with the dogs of war.

If humanity could be taught self-control
and selfishness-control, there would be
no need for atom control.

You are none the holier for being praised,
and none the worse for being blamed.

You can't get anywhere today if you are still
mired down in yesterday.

The load of tomorrow added to that of yesterday,
carried today, makes the strongest falter.

Worry is interest paid on trouble before it is due.

Reality may be a rough road, but escape
is a precipice.

Nothing in life is to be feared. It is only
to be understood.

He that goes a borrowing goes a sorrowing.

That man is the richest whose pleasures
are the cheapest.

The Bible is the book of all others to be read
at all ages and in all conditions of human life.

Work is the best narcotic.

Habit is man's best friend or his worst enemy.

Quiet minds cannot be perplexed or frightened
but go on in fortune or in misfortune at
their own private pace like the ticking of a
clock during a thunderstorm.

Our restlessness is largely due to the fact that we
are as yet wanderers between two worlds.

Who is wise? He that learns from everyone.
Who is powerful? He that governs his passions.
Who is rich? He that is content.
Who is that? Nobody.

The fellow who worries about what people
think of him wouldn't worry so much if he only
knew how seldom they do.

> Absence of occupation is not rest;
> A mind quite vacant is a mind distressed.

He only is advancing in life whose heart is
getting softer, his blood warmer, his brain
quicker, and his spirit entering into living peace.

No wise man ever wished to be younger.

A clean conscience is a soft pillow.

All the sleepless nights, burdened days, joyless,
restless, peace-destroying, health-destroying,
happiness-destroying, love-destroying hours men
and women have ever in all earth's centuries given
to Worry never wrought one good thing!

He who is taught to live upon little owes
more to his father's wisdom than he who has a
great deal left him does to his father's care.

When you can no longer dwell in the solitude
of your heart, you live in your lips and sound
is a diversion and a pastime.

> Worry never climbed a hill
> Worry never paid a bill
> Worry never dried a tear
> Worry never calmed a fear
> Worry never darned a heel
> Worry never cooked a meal
> Worry never led a horse to water
> Worry never done a thing you'd
>   think it oughta.

There is no conflict between the *old*
and the *new;* the conflict is between the
false and the *true.*

It's right to be contented with what you have
but never with what you are.

> There is no place to hide a sin,
> Without the conscience looking in!

Peace is not the absence of conflict, but the
ability to cope with it.

The rest of our days depends upon the
rest of our nights.

Anger is a wind which blows out
the lamp of the mind.

Though we travel the world over to find
the beautiful, we must carry it with us
or we find it not.

> Rest is not quitting the busy career;
> Rest is the fitting of self to its sphere.
> 'Tis loving and serving the highest and best!
> 'Tis onward unswerving, and that is true rest.

Are you disillusioned with your disillusionments?

Life is a voyage in which we choose
neither vessel nor weather, but much can
be done in the management of the sails and the
guidance of the helm.

A good memory is fine—but the ability to
forget is the true test of greatness.

The light that shows us our sin is the light
that heals us.

God grant me the serenity to accept the things
I cannot change; the courage to change the things
I can; and the wisdom to know the difference.

To will what God wills brings peace.

Climb the mountains and get their glad
tidings. Nature's peace will flow to you as
the sunshine flows into the trees. The winds blow
their own freshness into you, and the storms
their energy, while cares drop away from
you like the leaves of autumn.

Not even the perpetually hungry
live by bread alone.

Solitude is the ante-chamber of God;
only one step more and you will be in
His immediate presence.

Any housewife, no matter how large her
family, can always get some time to be alone
by doing the dishes.

Great people are not affected by each puff of
wind that blows ill. Like great ships, they sail
serenely on, in a calm sea or a great tempest.

If you have known how to compose your life,
you have accomplished a great deal more
than a man who knows how to compose a
book. Have you been able to take your stride?
You have done more than the man who
has taken cities and empires.

Meditation or Medication?

Pray or be a prey—a prey to fears,
to futilities. to ineffectiveness.

You talk when you cease to be at peace
with your thoughts.

A minute of thought is worth more than
an hour of talk.

The itching sensation that some people
mistake for ambition is merely inflammation
of the wishbone.

To be content with little is difficult, to be
content with much, impossible.

Long suffering

Much wisdom remains to be learned, and if
it is only to be learned through adversity,
we must endeavor to endure adversity with
what fortitude we can command. But if we
can acquire wisdom soon enough, adversity
may not be necessary and the future of man
may be happier than any part of his past.

Education is a companion which no misfortune
can decrease, no crime destroy, no enemy
alienate, no despotism enslave; at home a friend,
abroad an introduction, in solitude a solace,
in society an ornament. It chastens vice,
guides virtue, and gives grace and government
to genius. Education may cost financial
sacrifice and mental pain, but in both
money and life values it will repay every
cost one hundred fold.

There is a field for critics, no doubt, but we
don't remember seeing statues of any of them
in the Hall of Fame.

Why must we have memory enough to recall
to the tiniest detail what has happened to
us, and not enough to remember how many
times we have told it to the same person.

The bird with a broken pinion never soared
so high again, but its song is sweeter!

Whoever has resigned himself to fate,
will find that fate, accepts his resignation.

One of the hardest things to teach our children
about money matters is that it does.

> If you have learned to walk
> A little more sure-footedly than I,
> Be patient with my stumbling then
> And know that only as I do my best and try
> May I attain the goal
> For which we both are striving.
>
> If through experience, your soul
> Has gained heights which I
> As yet in dim-lit vision see,
> Hold out your hand and point the way,
> Lest from its straightness I should stray,
> And walk a mile with me.

Men and automobiles are much alike. Some are
right at home on an uphill pull; others run
smoothly only going down-grade, and when you
hear one knocking all the time, it's a sure sign
there is something wrong under the hood.

Charity is injurious unless it helps the
recipient to become independent of it.

We can do anything we want if we
stick to it long enough.

What we do not understand we do not possess.

Will Power—Won't Power—Supreme Power!

If you never stick your neck out, you'll
never get your head above the crowd.

Patience—in time the grass becomes milk.

There is no sense in advertising your troubles.
There's no market for them.

Genius is only patience.

He who accepts evil without protesting against it
is really cooperating with it.

A man could retire nicely in his old age
if he could dispose of his experience
for what it cost him.

It is not the ship in the water but the water
in the ship that sinks it.

It is not miserable to be blind; it is miserable
to be incapable of enduring blindness.

You cannot help men permanently by
doing for them what they could and should
do for themselves.

Fortune does not change men. It only
unmasks them.

Use disappointment as material for patience.

Telling your troubles always helps. The
world's dumb indifference makes you mad
enough to keep on fighting.

Women are here to stay . . .
let's make the best of them.

Those who have suffered much are like those
who know many languages; they have learned
to understand all and to be understood by all.

The worst thing that happens to a man
may be the best thing that ever happened to
him if he doesn't let it get the best of him.

There is no failure save in giving up.

Sometimes the best gain is to lose.

A man can fail many times, but he isn't a failure
until he begins to blame somebody else.

Forget mistakes. Organize victory out of mistakes.

All problems become smaller if you don't
dodge them but confront them. Touch a
thistle timidly and it will prick you; grasp
it boldly and its spines crumble.

He who strikes the first blow confesses
he has run out of ideas.

A man's best fortune or his worst is his wife.

When you're through changing, you're through.

The diamond cannot be polished without
friction, nor man perfected without trials.

Trying times are times for trying.

Education should be as gradual as the moon-
rise, perceptible not in progress but in result.

Why value the present hour less than
some future hour?

The secret of patience is doing something else
in the meanwhile.

If you don't scale the mountain, you
can't see the view.

Trouble is only opportunity in work clothes.

Only one person in the whole wide world
can defeat you. That is yourself!

> Like a hick'ry cog
> In the old mill wheel,
> He did his part
> As his turn came 'round.

I had no shoes and complained until I met
a man who had no feet.

Before you flare up at any one's faults, take
time to count ten—ten of your own.

We are never more discontented with others
than when we are discontented with ourselves.

The door to the room of success swings
on the hinges of opposition.

It isn't the load that weights us down—
it's the way we carry it.

The greatest calamity is not to have failed;
but to have failed to try.

The only time you mustn't fail is the
last time you try.

A diamond is a piece of coal that
stuck to the job.

God never makes us conscious of our weakness
except to give us of His strength.

There is nothing wrong with the younger gener-
ation that twenty years won't cure.

Stars may be seen from the bottom of
a deep well, when they cannot be seen from
the top of the mountain. So are many
things learned in adversity, which the
prosperous man dreams not of.

Perhaps the most valuable result of all
education is the *ability* to make ourselves do
the thing we have to do *when* it ought to be
done, whether we like it or not.

> The hardest thing of all in life—
>   The conquest not of time and space,
> But of ourselves, of our stupidity and inertia,
>   of our greediness and touchiness,
> Of our fear and intolerant dogmatism.

The difference between stumbling blocks and
stepping stones is the way a man uses them.

Every time you give another a 'piece of your
mind' you add to your own vacuum.

We cannot do everything at once; but
we can do something at once.

No horse gets anywhere till he is harnessed.
No steam ever drives anything
until it is confined.
No Niagara is ever turned into light and power
until it is tunneled.
No life ever grows great until it is focused,
dedicated, disciplined.

A mistake is evidence that someone has
tried to do something.

When the archer misses the center of the target
he seeks for the cause within himself.

The world is made better by every man
improving his own conduct; and no reform
is accomplished wholesale.

The most difficult year of marriage is the
one you're in.

Life is 10% what you make it and 90%
how you take it.

Be not angry that you cannot make others
as you wish them to be since you cannot make
yourself as you wish to be.

Itching for what you want doesn't do much
good; you've got to scratch for it.

He who has learned to disagree without being
disagreeable has discovered the most valuable
secret of a diplomat.

Your ulcers are not due to what you are eatin'
but to what's eatin' you.

Better to let 'em wonder why you didn't talk
than why you did.

We would rather be ruined by praise
than saved by criticism.

If at first you don't succeed, you are running
about average.

Do not be disturbed at being misunderstood.
Be disturbed only at not understanding.

> Our Country, right or wrong!
> When right, to be kept right;
> When wrong, to be put right.

You've reached middle age when all you
exercise is caution.

It takes the whole of life to learn how to live.

Housework is something you do that nobody
notices unless you don't do it.

It isn't the mountain ahead that wears you out—
it's the grain of sand in your shoe.

The highest reward that God gives us for
good work is the ability to do better.

Everything comes to him who waits, if he
works while he waits.

Injustice is relatively easy to bear;
what stings is justice.

Do not go to pieces if you burn the toast.
Some day your house may burn down and you
can take that calmly too.

Marrying is not Marriage.

No one can work me injury but myself.

To be thrown upon one's resources is to be cast
into the very lap of fortune.

The trouble with some people is
that they won't admit their faults.
I'd admit mine—if I had any.

The Lord sometimes takes us into troubled
waters NOT to drown us, but to cleanse us.

Try to fix the mistake—never the blame.

To sin by silence when they should protest,
makes cowards of men.

The world is not interested in the storms
you encountered—but did you bring in the ship?

> I'd better not be wasting Time,
>   For Time is wasting me!

Just about the time you think you can make
both ends meet, somebody moves the ends.

Education isn't play and it can't be made
to look like play. It is hard, hard work, but
it can be made interesting work.

Talent may develop in solitude, but character
is developed in society.

The more difficult the obstacle, the
stronger one becomes after hurdling it.

Tact is the ability to close your mouth
before someone else wants to.

Fault finders never improve the world; they
only make it seem worse than it really is.

Don't tell your friends about your *indigestion:*
'How are you' is a *greeting,* not a question.

> No difficulties, no discovery,
> No pains, no gains.

Taxes could be much worse—suppose we had
to pay on what we *think* we're worth.

A failure is a man who has blundered but is not
able to cash in the experience.

Failure is endeavor, and endeavor
persisted in, is never failure.

> One thing at a time and that done well
> is a very good rule as many can tell.

Help me never to judge another until I have
walked two weeks in his shoes.

Learn from the mistakes of others—you can't
live long enough to make them all yourself.

Gentleness

This book can be like a well-chosen and well-tended fruit tree. Its fruits are not of one season only. With the due and natural intervals, you may recur to it year after year, and it will supply the same nourishment and the same gratification, if only you return to it with the same healthy appetite.

> So many Gods, so many creeds,
> So many paths that wind and wind;
> When just the art of being kind
> Is all the sad world needs.

If you have a weakness, make it work for you as a strength—and if you have a strength, don't abuse it into a weakness.

The kindly word that falls today may bear its fruit tomorrow.

A good manner springs from a good heart, and fine manners are the outcome of unselfish kindness.

One cannot find any rule of conduct to excel 'simplicity' and 'sincerity.'

To speak kindly does not hurt the tongue.

Every noble life leaves the fibre of it interwoven in the woof of the world.

He who influences the thought of his time influences the thought of all the times that follow.

The blossom cannot tell what becomes of its odor and no man can tell what becomes of his influence and example that roll away from him and go beyond his view.

Only the best behavior is good enough for daily use in the home.

True nobility comes of the gentle heart.

Prejudice is being down on what we are not up on.

Nothing is so strong as gentleness, nothing so gentle as real strength.

A candle-glow can pierce the darkest night.

A gentleman is a gentle man.

Speech may sometimes do harm; but so may silence and a worse harm at that. No insult ever caused so deep a wound as a tenderness expected and withheld; and no spoken indiscretion was ever so bitterly regretted as the word that one did not speak.

Be what you wish others to become.

Kindness is a language the dumb can speak
and the deaf understand.

> Be to his virtues very kind.
> Be to his faults a little blind.

One learns manners from those who have none.

An admission of error is a sign of strength
rather than a confession of weakness.

If you confer a benefit, never remember it;
If you receive one, never forget it.

Be kind, for everyone you meet is
fighting a hard battle.

Goodness

We are all manufacturers, making goods,
making trouble or making excuses.

A little thing is a little thing, but faithfulness
in little things is a great thing.

Character is property—it is the noblest
of possessions.

The highest reward for a man's toil is not what
he gets for it, but rather what he becomes by it.

It is not so much what a man is descended from
that matters as what he will descend to.

Truth is the foundation of all knowledge
and the cement of all societies.

You can preach a better sermon with your life
than with your lips.

Praise not only pretends that we are
better than we are; it may help to make
us better than we are.

Good depends not on things but on the
use we make of things.

Resolve to be better for the echo of it.

If anyone speaks evil of you, so live
that none will believe it.

Life is too short to be little.

To the man in us, time is a quantity;
To the God in us, it is a quality.

To do the right thing for the wrong reason
is the greatest treason.

> Who worships Christ in bread and wine,
>   And kneels before the High and Pure,
> Meets Him again in street and mine
>   And in the faces of the poor.

We've got to build a better man before
we build a better society.

> You are writing a gospel,
> A chapter each day,
> By deeds that you do,
> By words that you say.
> Men read what you write,
> Whether faithless or true,
> Say, what is the gospel according to you?

The only way to settle a disagreement is
on the basis of what's right—not who's right.

What I must do, and not what people think,
is all that concerns me.

Silver and gold are not the only coin; virtue
also passes all over the world.

Your luck is how you treat people.

The measure of man's real character
is what he would do if he knew he would
never be found out.

See each person you meet as one who knows
your Lord or is seeking your Lord.

To every man there opens a high way and a low
and every man decides the way that he shall go.

> We search the world for truth, we cull
> The good, the true, the beautiful,
> From graven stone and written scroll,
> And all old flower-fields of the soul;
> And, weary seekers of the best,
> We come back laden from our quest,
> To find that all the sages said
> Is in the Book our mothers read.

We have committed the Golden Rule to memory;
let us now commit it to life.

The greatest distance we have yet to cover
still lies within us.

A man is rich according to what he is,
not according to what he has.

A good example is the best sermon.

The world is slowly learning that because two
men think differently neither need be wicked.

The Golden Rule—not the rule of gold.

Children need models more than they need critics.

Life lived just to satisfy yourself never
satisfies anybody.

There is no better exercise for strengthening the
heart than reaching down and lifting people up.

What lies behind us and what lies before us are
tiny matters compared to what lies within us.

Character is a victory, not a gift.

There is no right way to do the wrong thing.

Whatever creed be taught or land be trod,
Man's conscience is the oracle of God.

What I am to be I am now becoming.

The hardest job that people have to do is to
move religion from their throats to their muscles.

A living religion is a way of living.

A man's reputation is only what men think him
to be; his character is what God knows him to be.

Goodness is the only investment that never fails.

Though another may have more money, beauty,
brains than you; yet when it comes to the rarer
spiritual values such as charity, self-sacrifice,
honor, nobility of heart, you have an equal
chance with everyone to be the most beloved
and honored of all people.

The real purpose of our existence is not to
make a living, but to make a life—a worthy,
well-rounded, useful life.

> Do all the good you can
> By all the means you can
> In all the ways you can
> In all the places you can
> At all the times you can
> To all the people you can
> As long as ever you can.

Christian character is not an inheritance; each
individual must build it for himself.

What you are in the sight of God,
that you truly are.

To clear difficulties out of the way, there is
no axe like a good principle.

Are you easing the load of overtaxed
lifters who toil down the road? Or, are you a
leaner who lets others share your portion
of labor, worry and care?

Good nature will always supply the
absence of beauty; but beauty cannot supply
the absence of good nature.

Be careful how you live; you may be the
only Bible some people will ever read.

Be the true man you seek.

Nothing which is morally wrong can
ever be politically right.

My part is to improve the present moment.

Do right and leave the results with God.

The difference between a prejudice and a
conviction is that you can explain a conviction
without getting mad.

To become Christlike is the only thing in the
whole world worth caring for; the thing
before which every ambition of man is folly,
and all lower achievement vain.

It will not be easy to brainwash the heartwashed.

Democracy means not 'I am equal to you'
but 'you are equal to me.'

Life is not the wick or the candle—it is the burning.

It is often surprising to find what heights may
be attained merely by remaining on the level.

It is as hard for the good to suspect evil
as it is for the bad to suspect good.

> For when the One Great Scorer comes,
>   To write against your name,
> He writes not that you lost or won,
>   But how you played the game.

All that is necessary for the triumph of evil is
that good men do nothing.

The Devil has many tools, but a lie is
the handle that fits them all.

Know enough to, know enough not to.

If you blame others for your failures,
do you credit others with your successes?

There isn't any map on the *road* to *success;*
you have to find your own way.

He who is not liberal with what he has
deceives himself when he thinks he would
be liberal if he had more.

Are you trying to make something for yourself
or something of yourself?

A lie has no legs. It requires other lies to
support it. Tell one lie and you are forced
to tell others to back it up.

A good man does not hesitate to own he has been
in the wrong. He takes comfort in knowing
he is wiser today than he was yesterday.

Stretching the truth won't make it last any longer.

The only wise speed at which to live
is . . . Godspeed.

I have resolved never to do anything
which I should be afraid to do if it were
the last hour of my life.

Faith

Faith is a gift of God. It is not a material that
can be seen, heard, smelled, tasted, or touched;
but is as real as anything that can be perceived
with these senses. One can be aware of
Faith as easily as one can be aware of earth.
Faith is as certain as is the existence of water.
Faith is as sure as the taste of an apple, the
fragrance of a rose, the sound of thunder,
the sight of the sun, the feel of a loving touch.
Hope is a wish, a longing for something not now
possessed, but with the expectation of getting it.
Faith adds surety to the expectation of hope.

Today is the tomorrow you worried about yesterday.

I am to be so busy today that I must spend
more time than usual in prayer.

Inexperience is what makes a young man do
what an older man says is impossible.

When you get to the end of your rope,
tie a knot in it and hang on.

You are not a reservoir with a limited
amount of resources; you are a channel attached
to unlimited divine resources.

God is playing chess with man. He meets
his every move.

The sectarian thinks that he has the sea ladled
into his private pond.

Who draws nigh to God through doubtings dim . . .
God will advance a mile in blazing light to him.

I am only one, but I am one. I cannot
do everything, but I can do something;
and what I should do and can do, by the
Grace of God I will do.

> No vision and you perish
>   No ideal and you are lost,
> Your heart must ever cherish
>   Some faith at any cost.

Anyone can carry his burden, however heavy,
until nightfall; anyone can do his work,
however hard, for one day.

Prayer is not overcoming God's reluctance; it is
laying hold on His willingness.

Prayer is not an attitude attained but an
attitude maintained.

The secret of prayer is secret prayer.

The man who trusts men will make fewer
mistakes than he who distrusts them.

God's requirements are met by God's enablings.

A skeptic is one who won't take *know*
for an answer.

I have faith in Him, not in my faith.

No man is responsible for the rightness of his
faith; but only for the uprightness of it.

Dare to be wise; begin! He who postpones the
hour of living rightly is like the rustic who waits
for the river to run out before he crosses.

The night is not forever.

Do not worry about whether or not the sun
will rise; be prepared to enjoy it.

The best and most beautiful things
in the world cannot be seen nor touched
but are felt in the heart.

The Christian on his knees sees more than the
philosopher on tiptoe.

Nothing costs so much as what is bought by prayers.

It is better to suffer wrong than to do it, and
happier to sometimes be cheated than not to trust.

God never closes one door without opening another.

Faith is the grave of care.

Prayer is not a substitute for work. It is a
desperate effort to work further and to be
effective beyond the range of one's power.

We are always complaining our days are
few, and acting as though there would be
no end of them.

The past cannot be changed; the future is
still in your power.

O, Lord, help me to understand that you ain't
gwine to let nuthin' come my way that you
and me together can't handle.

> What you can do, or dream you can, begin it.
> Courage has genius, power and magic in it;
> Only engage, and then the mind grows heated.
> Begin it and the work will be completed.

Some people can see at a glance what others
cannot see with searchlights and telescopes.

The best evidence of the Bible's being the Word
of God is to be found between its covers.

Life is easier than you think. All you have to
do is accept the impossible, do without the
indispensable, and bear the intolerable.

> Prayer without work is beggary;
> Work without prayer is slavery.

What are you saving in your memory bin
as food for the restless soul when the
winter of life comes?

I'll take the Bible as my guide until something
better comes along.

For a web begun, God sends thread.

Life is eternal, Love is immortal and Death
is only an horizon, and an horizon is only
the limit of our sight.

Instead of waiting upon the Lord, some people
want the Lord to wait upon them.

> This body is my house—it is not I.
> Triumphant in this faith I live and die.

Satan trembles when he sees the weakest saint
upon his knees.

To pray 'Thy will be done' should be no
attitude of passive submission but a call to the
whole nature to strive to do the utmost for
the cause of God.

> With God, go even over the sea;
> Without Him, not over the threshold.

With God, nothing shall be impossible.

It is not the lazy who are most inclined
to prayer; those pray most who care most,
and who, having worked hard, find it intolerable
to be defeated.

Don't tell me that worry doesn't do any
good. I know better. The things I worry about
don't happen.

If a man has any religion, he must give it up
or give it away.

Do the very best you can . . .
and leave the outcome to God.

I know not what the future hath of marvel
or surprise, assured alone that life and death
His mercy underlies.

> The trival round, our common task,
>   Would furnish all we ought to ask;
> Room to deny ourselves; a road
>   to bring us daily nearer God.

Real prayer always does one of two things:
It either frees us from the trouble we fear or
else it gives us the strength and courage to
meet the trouble when it comes.

One on God's side is a majority.

Are your troubles causing you to lose your
religion or use your religion?

Wit's end need not be the end, but the
beginning. The end of man's contriving often
is the beginning of God's arriving.

Life left to God
Will bring a greater yield
Of golden harvest and of ripened field
Than all the weary plannings of thy soul
Can force to be, or strength of will control;
Oh, trust a Power that must bring good from all,
And leave thy life to God!

If a psychologist assures me that I believe in
God because of the way my nurse used to treat
me, I must reply that he only holds that belief
concerning my belief because of the way in
which his nurse used to treat him.

Why is it opportunities always look bigger
going than coming?

All I see teaches me to trust the Creator for
all I do not see.

If seeds in the black earth can turn into such
beautiful roses, what might not the heart of man
become in its long journey toward the stars?

> Of all the troubles great and small
> are those that never happened at all.

The Bible is a guidebook; the way to master it
is to let it master us.

Freedom rests, and always will, on
individual responsibility, individual integrity,
individual effort, individual courage, and
individual religious faith.

Man's extremity is God's opportunity.

If there is no way out, there is a way up.

This is what I found out about religion:
It gives you courage to make the decisions
you must make in a crisis, and then the
confidence to leave the result to a *higher
power.* Only by trust in God can a man carrying
responsibility find repose.

A wish is a desire without any attempt to
attain its end.

It is difficult to pray because it is difficult to
know what we ought to desire.

It is only the fear of God that can deliver us
from the fear of men.

Morale is when your hands and feet keep
on working when your head says it can't be done.

Death is not extinguishing the light; it is putting
out the lamp because dawn has come.

> Out of the seed the flower;
>   Out of the flower the seed;
> Out of the need the power;
>   Out of the power the deed.

Only he who can see the invisible can
do the impossible.

> Do you pray, and then believing,
>   Grab your boots and parasol;
> Scrub the barrel and *get ready*
>   For the rain you asked to fall?

Don't be afraid to be afraid.

He says not, 'at the end of the *way* you
find ME.' He says, 'I AM the *way*: I AM the
road under your feet, the road that begins
just as low as you happen to be.'

Be patient enough to live one day at a time
as Jesus taught us, letting yesterday go and
leaving tomorrow until it arrives.

Instead of fearing death, we should look it
in the face and recognize it for what it is—
a friend that has come to release us from the
bondage of the flesh.

Lord, I shall be very busy this day. I may
forget thee . . . But do not Thou forget me.

We plant a tree this day and leave the
blossoming to God.

Fear brings more pain than does the pain it fears.

All the fitness He requireth is to feel
your need of Him.

Does your faith move mountains, or do
mountains move your faith?

Prayer should be the key of the day and the
lock of the night.

Do you have invisible means of support?

Our doubts are traitors and make us lose the good
oft we might win, by fearing to attempt.

> Life is real! Life is earnest!
> And the grave is not its goal;
> Dust thou art, to dust returnest,
> Was not spoken of the soul.

If you must doubt, doubt your doubts—
never your beliefs.

A man is not old until regrets
take the place of dreams.

Cease to inquire what the future has in store,
but take as a gift whatever the day brings forth.

Nothing is all wrong. Even a clock that has
stopped running is right twice a day.

No worlds left to conquer? The frontiers of
the mind are just beginning to be discovered,
and the spiritual world surrounding us yet
remains a complete mystery.

First do more than you are paid for before
expecting to be paid for more than you do.

Prayer digs the channels from the reservoir
of God's boundless resources to the tiny pools
of our lives.

There is no greater obstacle in the way
of success in life than trusting for something
to turn up, instead of going to work and
turning up something.

> I never knew a night so black
> Light failed to follow on its track.
> I never knew a storm so gray,
> It failed to have its clearing day.
> I never knew such bleak despair,
> That there was not a rift, somewhere.
> I never knew an hour so drear,
> Love could not fill it full of cheer.

Some folks just don't seem to realize when
they're moaning about not getting prayers
answered, that NO is the answer.

> Life is hard, by the yard;
> But by the inch, *life's* a cinch!

The task of spiritual science: Discover the
little acorns out of which big oaks grow and
provide room for the growth of such mighty trees.

We can easily forgive a child who is afraid
of the dark. The real tragedy of life is when
men are afraid of the Light.

> Without the *way*, there is no going;
> Without the *truth*, there is no knowing;
> Without the *life,* there is no living.

The world is moved not only by the mighty
shoves of the heroes, but also by the aggregate
of the tiny pushes of each honest worker.

He didn't know it couldn't be done
but went ahead and did it.

> A Traveler crossed a frozen stream
>   In trembling fear one day;
> Later a teamster drove across,
>   And whistled all the way.

> Great faith and little faith alike
>   Were granted safe convoy;
> One had the pangs of needless fear,
>   The other all the joy.

It is not the greatness of my faith that moves
mountains, but my faith in the greatness of God.

You can't control the length of your life—but
you can control its width and depth. You can't
control the contour of your face—but you
can control its expression. You can't control the
weather—but you can control the atmosphere
of your mind. Why worry about things you
can't control when you can keep yourself
busy controlling the things that depend on you.

People believe what they want to believe
despite all the evidence to the contrary.

As is your 'Amen' so is your prayer.

Prayer changes things. Prayer changes you!

> He who loses money loses much;
> he who loses a friend loses more,
> but he who loses *faith* loses all.

The only ideas that will work for you are the
ones you put to work.

> God without man is still God.
> Man without God is nothing.

When we see the lilies spinning in distress,
Taking thought to manufacture loveliness—
When we see the birds all building barns for store,
'Twill be time for us to worry, not before.

Meekness

Have courage to be ignorant of a great
number of things, in order to avoid the calamity
of being ignorant of everything.

The only conquests which are permanent, and
leave no regrets, are conquests over ourselves.

Resiliency is an important factor in living.
The winds of life may bend us, but if we have
resilience of spirit, they cannot break us.
To courageously straighten again after our heads
have been bowed by defeat, disappointment
and suffering is the supreme test of character.

To know how to grow old is the master
work of wisdom, and one of the most difficult
chapters in the great art of living.

The best medicine for you to take is yourself—
with a grain of salt.

It is with narrow-souled people as with
narrow necked bottles—the less they have in
them the more noise they make in pouring it out.

There is only one person with whom
you can profitably compare yourself, and this
person is your yesterday self: You.

The greatest undeveloped territory in the world
lies under your hat.

Discussion is an exchange of knowledge:
argument is an exchange of ignorance.

Wisdom is to know what is best worth knowing
and to do what is best worth doing.

Some husbands know all the answers. They've
been listening for years.

If we resist our passions, it is more through
their weakness than our strength.

Conscience is the still small voice that makes
you feel still smaller.

The doorstep to the temple of wisdom is a
knowledge of our own ignorance.

To be conscious that you are ignorant is
a great step toward knowledge.

Never forget that you are a part of the people
who can be fooled some of the time.

Don't drive as if you own the road; Drive as
if you own the car.

Teach thy tongue to say, 'I do not know.'

A juvenile delinquent is a boy who does what
you did when young, but gets caught.

There is nothing permanent but change.

The best way to succeed in life is to act on the
advice you give to others.

A peck of common sense is worth
a bushel of learning.

The bigger a man's head gets, the easier it is
to fill his shoes.

Past experience should be a guide post,
not a hitching post.

The end of wisdom is to dream high enough
not to lose the dream in the seeking of it.

There's nothing wrong with being a self-made man
if you don't consider the job finished too soon.

The aim of education is to enable man
to continue his learning.

Life is like a ladder. Every step we take is
either up or down.

What a fool does in the end, the wise man
does in the beginning.

A college education seldom hurts a man
if he's willing to learn a little something
after he graduates.

Swallowing your pride occasionally will never
give you indigestion.

A philosopher is someone who always knows
what to do until it happens to him.

I am not conceited, though I do have every reason to be.

The steam that blows the whistle can't be used to turn the wheels.

Manhood, not scholarship, is the first aim of education.

When success turns a person's head, he is facing failure.

Men are wise in proportion not to their experience but to their capacity for experience.

No experienced man ever stigmatized a change of opinion as inconsistency.

Education does not mean teaching people to know what they do not know; it means teaching them to behave as they do not behave.

Quite often when a man thinks his mind is getting broader it is only his conscience stretching.

Opinions that are well rooted should grow and change like a healthy tree.

Lord, give me this day my daily opinion, and forgive me the one I had yesterday.

I thoroughly believe in a university education for both men and women, but I believe a knowledge of the Bible without a college course is more valuable than a college course without a knowledge of the Bible.

Many might have attained wisdom had they
not thought that they had already attained it.

The taller a bamboo grows, the lower it bends.

A criminal is nothing else but you and me at
our weakest, found out.

Seems as if some people grow with
responsibility—others just swell.

Every man I meet is in some way my superior;
and in that I can learn from him.

When you know a thing, to hold that you
know it, and when you do not know it, to admit
that you do not—this is true knowledge.

The more you know, the more you know
you don't know.

To admit I have been in the wrong
is but saying that I am wiser today than
I was yesterday.

It makes a man sort of humble to have
been a kid when everything was the kid's
fault and a parent at a time when everything
is the parent's fault.

> The greatest friend of truth is time,
> And her constant companion is humility.

When you hear that someone has
gossiped of you, kindly reply that he did not
know the rest of your faults or he would not
have mentioned only these.

To err may be human, but to admit it isn't.

The purpose of education is to provide
everyone with the opportunity to learn how
best he may serve the world.

Nothing gives a man more leisure time
than being punctual.

A professor once said that it didn't
matter if one said, "I seed," if one really
had seen something.

Wisdom consists in knowing what to do
with what you know.

A learned man has always wealth within himself.

Investment in knowledge pays the best interest.

The man who trims himself to suit everybody
will soon whittle himself away.

The righteous cannot rise beyond the highest
which is in me so the wicked and the
weak cannot fall lower than the lowest in me.

Everyone is ignorant—only on different subjects.

Humility is a strange thing. The minute
you think you've got it, you've lost it.

When young, consider that one day
you will be old and when old, remember
you were once young.

A man wrapped up in himself makes
a very small bundle.

They that know God will be humble;
they that know themselves cannot be proud.

If you want to put the world right,
start with yourself.

It is indeed a desirable thing
to be well descended, but the glory
belongs to our ancestors.

A college graduate is a person who had a
chance to get an education.

Tolerance comes with age. I see no fault
committed that I myself could not have
committed at some time or other.

The greatest of faults is to be conscious of none.

Nonchalance is the ability to look like an owl
when you have acted like a jackass.

When a man gets too old to set a bad example,
he starts giving good advice.

An open mind leaves a chance for someone to
drop a worthwhile thought in it.

A diplomat is one who can tell a man
he's open minded when he means he has a
hole in his head.

We see things not as they are, but as we are.

The best thing for gray hair is a sensible head.

Time cannot be expanded, accumulated,
mortgaged, hastened, or retarded.

Women will remain the weaker sex just as long as they're smarter.

It is my privilege to profit by the experience of others, but I must live my own life, face the trials, and gain the victory alone.

God never makes us sensible of our weakness except to give us of His strength.

Most people's hindsight is 20/20.

Every other kind of iniquity prompts the doing of evil deeds, but pride lurks even in good deeds to their undoing.

> Are you sure that you are Right?
>   How fine and strong!
> But were you ever just as sure—
>   And wrong?

Flattery is something nice someone tells you about yourself that you wish were true.

It is better to understand a little than to misunderstand a lot.

Temperance

Where there is an open mind, there will
always be a frontier.

The longer you keep your temper the more
it will improve.

It's smart to pick your friends—but not to pieces.

Fine eloquence consists in saying all that
should be, not all that could be said.

Wise men are not always silent, but know
when to be.

We always have time enough
if we but use it aright.

Spend less than you get.

Frugality is good if liberality be joined by it.

It's not that I spend more than I earn, it's just
that I spend it quicker than I earn it.

There is only a slight difference between
keeping your chin up and sticking your neck
out, but it's worth knowing.

The hand that lifts 'the cup that cheers' should
not be used to shift the gears.

> The driver is safer when the roads are dry;
> the roads are safer when the driver is dry.

Be sure your brain is in gear
before engaging your mouth.

Blessed is he who, having nothing to say,
refrains from giving wordy evidence of the fact.

If your dollar won't do as much as it once
did, consider: Are you doing as much as
you once did for a dollar?

Laziness travels so slowly that poverty soon
overtakes him.

A man's difficulties begin when he is able to
do as he likes.

We cannot do everything at once;
but we can do something at once.

As easy as falling off a diet.

Gossip is the art of saying nothing
in a way that leaves nothing unsaid.

Words in haste do friendships waste.

Silence is a talent as greatly to be cherished
as that other asset, the gift of speech.

'A soft answer turneth away wrath' is the best
system of self-defense.

People who fly into a rage always make
a bad landing.

I'se alus mighty careful to stop and taste mah
words 'fore I lets 'em pass mah teeth!

Often the difference between a successful
marriage and a mediocre one consists of
leaving about three or four things a day unsaid.

Will power is the ability to eat one salted peanut.

We need mental separators that take off the
few ounces of cream which are fit to be
spoken to others.

Tact is the unsaid part of what you think.

In any controversy the instant we feel anger we
have already ceased striving for truth, and have
begun striving for ourselves.

Thrift is a wonderful virtue—especially in ancestors.

It is better to keep your mouth shut and
thought a fool than it is to open it and prove it.

The best victory is to conquer self.

Dignity is the capacity to hold back on the
tongue what never should have been in the
mind in the first place.

To cease smoking is the easiest thing I ever did.
I ought to know for I've done it a thousand times.

Habit is a cable; we weave a thread of it
every day, and at last we cannot break it.

Choose the best life, for habit will make it pleasant.

Seconds count, especially when dieting.

The test of good manners is being able to
put up pleasantly with bad ones.

In times of crisis we must avoid both ignorant
change and ignorant opposition to change.

Best rule I know for talkin' is the same as the one
for carpenterin': Measure twice and saw once.

Even moderation ought not to be
practiced to excess.

Out of the mouths of babes come words we
shouldn't have said in the first place.

You can never tell about a woman, and if you
can, you shouldn't.

Who gossips to you will gossip of you.

The real problem of your leisure is how to keep
other people from using it.

Better to slip with the foot than with the tongue.

The archer who overshoots his mark does no
better than he who falls short of it.

Economy is an important virtue and debt
can be a danger to be feared.

Besides the noble art of getting things done,
there is the noble art of leaving things undone.
The wisdom of life consists in the elimination
of nonessentials.

Do you act or react?

We always weaken what we exaggerate.

There is nothing wrong with making mistakes,
but don't respond to encores.

Your body is for use—not abuse.

If silence be good for wise men, how much
better must it be for fools.

Do you spend more than you make on things you
don't need to impress people you don't like?

No echoes return to mock the silent tongue.

I have often regretted my speech,
seldom my silence.

It's all right to hold a conversation, but you
should let go of it now and then.

If your outgo exceeds your income, then your
upkeep will be your downfall.

Man is master of the unspoken word, which,
spoken, is master of him.

Speech is the index of the mind.

Overweight is often just desserts.

Money may not go as far as it used to, but we have just as much trouble getting it back.

A loose tongue often gets into a tight place.

Too many people quit looking for work when they find a job.

Ideas are funny little things. They won't work unless you do.

Sooner throw a pearl at hazard than an idle or useless word; and do not say a little in many words, but a great deal in a few.

Everything has been thought of before ...
the difficulty is to think of it again.